This journal holds the
fabulous writings of:
Carmen Flatt
2020

How would you describe your style?

Design your dream closet.

Your school announces that it will be changing the dress code next year. Explain what you think it should be and why.

Design a Halloween costume.
Draw it and/or describe it here.

Describe your personal style in five words or phrases!

Describe your favorite accessory. Where and when did you get it?

What kind of hat (baseball cap, knit cap, top hat, cowboy hat, etc.) represents each of your best friends. Why?

If you could only wear one color for an entire year, what color would it be, and why?

Draw a picture of your favorite shoes.
What makes them so perfect?

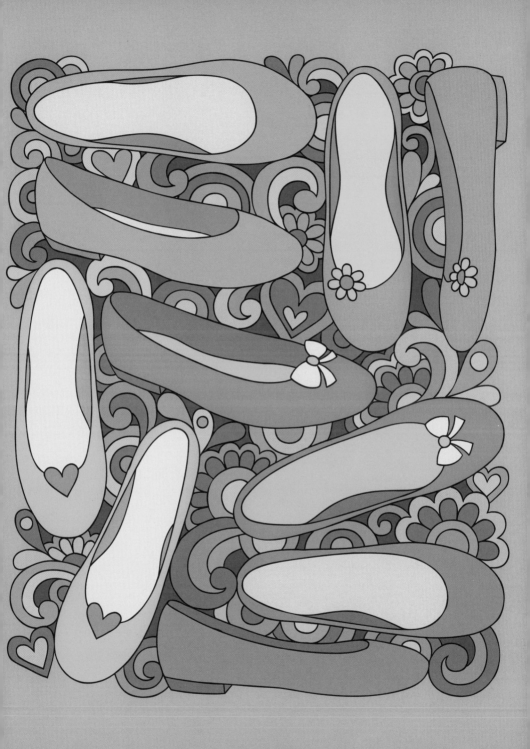

Your school needs a new mascot and team colors. What should they be, and why?

Find a picture of a historical figure you admire. Describe that person in words, using enough detail that someone who wasn't looking at the picture could know who it is.

Explain how you do your hair for school.

Find a picture of someone your age from one hundred years ago. How are your outfits alike? Different?

Decorate the patches and buttons
with your own doodle designs!

Your best friend is ready for a new winter look.
Design a cute outfit that will keep them warm.

Think of a type of art (like sculpture, weaving, or origami) that you've never tried. Write a letter to your art teacher explaining why your class should try it out.

Find a photo of a painting that inspires you.
What do you love about it?

Design an outfit that you could make out of things around the house, like plastic tablecloths or cloth napkins.

Explain how to do a load of laundry, step by step.

How does the color yellow make you feel? Are there any other colors that make you feel a certain way? What colors make you happy?

Make a plan to sew or create something new to wear or decorate your room. What materials will you need? How will you make it?

Design an awesome pair of socks your best friend would love to wear.

Decorate the sunglasses with your own patterns!

Write a letter to your parents persuading them to let you paint your bedroom a different color.

Describe an outfit that makes you feel absolutely amazing when you wear it. Where and when did you get it?

Draw an outline of your bedroom. Then cut out paper pieces for each piece of furniture. Place them in different arrangements in the room. Should you rearrange your room based on this model?

Tell the story of a time you did a good deed.

Think of a movie you've seen that was based on a book you've read. Was the movie or book better? Why?

What superpower would be perfect for you, and why?

Write a short story starting with this sentence:
It was a steep hill, but we'd made it.

Design a superhero outfit for yourself.

Design a doodled dress that you would love to wear!

Tell the story of a time you
solved a problem at home.

What are you really good at doing?

What is a skill you would like to learn?
How are you going to learn it?

Design an animal-themed outfit. Draw it here.

Imagine that you are running for class president. Write a speech convincing your classmates to vote for you.

Describe two of your past birthdays.
How were they different based on the
age you were turning?

Describe your locker, backpack, or bedroom. What does it say about you?

Create a fabulous piece of jewelry out of an unexpected object. Draw or describe it here.

Decorate these cute purses with your own doodle designs!

Tell the story of a time you made a cool piece of art.

Describe two different hairstyles that you have had.

What is one vintage item you wish would come back in style? Why?

Write a short story starting with this sentence: Jacob was up early enough to watch the sun rise, but he didn't.

Go through your closet and find something you haven't worn in a while. Draw and/or describe it here.

Tell the story of when and where you got your favorite accessory (like a backpack, pair of glasses, or piece of jewelry).

What type of art do you like the most?
Is it a painting, sculpture, drawing, dance,
music, or something else?

Draw a poster advertising the next school dance.

Customize the jeans with your own doodle decorations!

Do you have any bad habits you'd like to get rid of? Name good ones you'd like to have.

Ask someone you know for the story of how they got their pet. Retell it here.

Pick one item in your room and describe all the details: size, color, shape, texture, etc.

Design your own fabric pattern. Imagine it as a piece of clothing or something for your bedroom.

Design an outfit to wear to a school dance. Draw it and/or describe it here.

Design an outfit to wear for camping.
Draw it and/or describe it here.

Where would you rather be—in the mountains or at the beach? Why?

Describe how you look in words, as if you were a character being introduced in a book.

Doodle your favorite shoes from your closet
(or design your own amazing creations)!

Explain how to play your favorite game.

If you could take a month-long vacation to anywhere on Earth, where would it be, and why?

What's the silliest goal you've ever achieved?
What's the hardest goal you've achieved?

Find some images of hairstyles from the past. Should any come back in style? Which ones definitely should not?

Write a short story starting with this sentence: We had never noticed the box on the top shelf of the coat closet before.

What is your favorite holiday? Why?

Describe the street you live on. What's nice about it? What could be better?

Tell the story of a time when you were totally surprised by something.

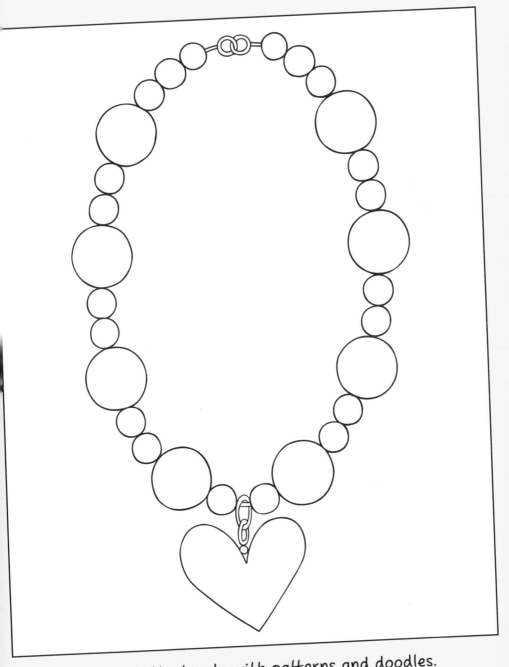

Decorate the beads with patterns and doodles.
Then add your own matching bracelet, ring, and earrings!

List five of your favorite things (phone, books, jewelry, etc.) and explain why they're important to you.

What are three things you never leave home without when you go to school? Why?

Write a short story starting with this sentence:
Emily chose the door on the left.

# About the Artist

Jess Volinski is a graduate of the School of Visual Arts in New York, NY, and the author/illustrator of more than a dozen coloring and activity books, including *Notebook Doodles® Super Cute*, *Notebook Doodles® Go Girl!*, and *Notebook Doodles® Sweets & Treats*. Besides creating books, she currently licenses her art for the publishing, fashion, and tableware industries. Originally from Connecticut, Jess now lives in southern New Jersey with her husband and two kids.

# Notebook Doodles® Activity Books

ISBN 978-1-64178-071-1

Fox Chapel Publishing makes every effort to use environmentally friendly paper for printing.

© 2019 by Jess Volinski and Quiet Fox Designs, *www.QuietFoxDesigns.com*, an imprint of Fox Chapel Publishing Company, Inc., 903 Square Street, Mount Joy, PA 17552.

We are always looking for talented authors and artists. To submit an idea, please send a brief inquiry to acquisitions@foxchapelpublishing.com.

Printed in China
First printing